ASK THIRD
WAY CAFÉ

Published in association with
Third Way Media, formerly
Mennonite Media

ASK THIRD WAY CAFÉ

50 Common and Quirky Questions About Mennonites

Jodi Nisly Hertzler

Foreword by Donald B. Kraybill

Publishing House
Telford, Pennsylvania

copublished with
Herald Press
Scottdale, Pennsylvania

Cascadia Publishing House LLC orders, information, reprint permissions:
contact@cascadiapublishinghouse.com
1-215-723-9125
126 Klingerman Road, Telford PA 18969
www.CascadiaPublishingHouse.com

Library of Congress Cataloguing-in-Publication Data
Hertzler, Jodi Nisly, 1973-
Ask Third Way Café : 50 common and quirky questions
about Mennonites / Jodi Nisly Hertzler.
p. cm.
Summary: "Collecting 50 of the questions about Mennonites the Third Way Café website has received over the years, this
book records the answers." "[summary]"--Provided by publisher.
ISBN-13: 978-1-931038-66-9 (trade pbk. : alk. paper)
ISBN-10: 1-931038-66-X (trade pbk. : alk. paper)
1. Mennonites--Doctrines. I. Title.

BX8121.3.H48 2009
230'.97--dc22

2009028201

16 15 13 12 11 10 09   10 9 8 7 6 5 4 3 2 1

*To Shelby, whose unique point of view and
sense of humor are invaluable in helping me process
tough questions;*

*and in memory of Erma Hess Brunk,
whose answers I still frequently refer to.*

CONTENTS

Chapter Three: Are Mennonites Allowed to Fight People Who Attack Them? 45

Chapter Four: Why Do They Live the Way They Do? 54

Chapter Five: Would It be Okay if I Became a Mennonite? 69

FOREWORD

Cheers for the folks at Third Way Café! They host a website that provides information and answers questions about all things Mennonite—responding to queries posed by the customers who chat at this cyber coffee shop.

Jodi Nisly Hertzler, who crafts answers for the flood of questions, keeps a fascinating log of the queries and how she responds. Neither she nor any other Mennonite has a Ph.D. in questionology, but she has a great gift of explaining what Mennonites think about almost anything—flags, sacraments, abortion, and even how to get to heaven. Some of Hertzler's answers are little tweets while others flow in succinct paragraphs, but regardless of length, they quickly capture Mennonite views on many things.

Some of the questions probe complicated theological doctrines about how creation happened, what really occurs at death, and whether Mennonites think they will go to purgatory. Others focus on Mennonite customs such as holidays and the holy kiss. Yes, the HOLY KISS. Still others strike at the very essence of things—are Mennonites permitted to marry? The YES to marriage was, I'm sure, not only the tweest tweet, but surely the easiest of all the queries.

It's no wonder that the questions visitors bring to the Third Way Café cover a vast cultural terrain because Mennonites indeed are a complicated, multi-textured people. A few drive horse and buggy, others ride in BMWs, and many just buy ordinary Camrys. Some of the more conservative folks in the Mennonite fold forbid television or using the Internet, but the vast majority of Mennonites tap modern technology with few blinks of reservation. Some own software companies and many are at home with iPods and texting.

Although most Mennonites speak English, the mother tongue of some of them living in North American is Vietnamese, Korean, Chinese, Spanish, or Pennsylvania German. Some attend Ivy League colleges while others end their formal schooling at the door of a one room school with eight grades. No wonder onlookers are baffled about and bedazzled by these folks who derive their name from Menno Simons, a former Catholic priest who joined the Anabaptist movement in Holland in 1536.

This interesting book does three things. It gives us a glimpse of the kind of questions about Mennonites that flash on the monitor of modern minds. It also shows the perceptions that circulate in the larger culture, what onlookers think about the Mennonite world. Perhaps most importantly, it provides a brief handbook regarding what Mennonites think and believe about a host of topics.

Mennonite readers will surely learn some new things about their own community. And their non-Mennonite neighbors around the world will find here an easy and fascinating read about all things Mennonite. So grab a cup of your favorite brew and join me raising our cups and cheers to Jodi Nisly Hertzler's fine efforts to pull all of these things together so succinctly and so well!

—*Donald B. Kraybill, author of* The Upside-Down Kingdom
and Senior Fellow, The Young Center, Elizabethtown College

Author's Preface

"Can you just send me everything there is to know . . . within reason?"

Seven years ago, Mennonite Media called with an intriguing proposal. They were looking for someone to work from home, answering questions generated by visitors to the Third Way Café website, the official website about and for Mennonites maintained by Mennonite Media, now Third Way Media, a mission of Mennonite Mission Network for Mennonite Church USA.

As a full-time mom and former English major, I had both the time and inclination to do some writing from my home. I don't profess to be an expert on Mennonites, but having grown up in the Anabaptist tradition, and having graduated from both a Mennonite high school and college, I know the basics. It didn't take long for me to learn that most people who write to us are just looking for a real person to communicate with. The Internet is an excellent medium in which to informally and anonymously ask questions, and our goal is to answer them in a similar vein—straight-up, brief, and "real."

We do have experts on standby should I get questions that delve into the highly theological or require relatively detailed or esoteric history. But I've found for the most part that people are just curious about Mennonites for a variety of reasons and are happy with fairly simple, informal answers.

These questions run a complete and often baffling gamut. Many are from students who need help with research. Prime examples: "I am doing a speech and I need some informachion (sic)" or "in paragraph form tell me who they are, where they came from, their culture, what they do as a group or culture, their religion, Thank you very much, please e-mail me as soon as possible, maybe tomorrow, but please soon. The fate of humanity is in your hands." I generally refer these folks to the appropriate areas on the Third Way Café website, which is comprehensive enough to cover most queries. Some students are a bit more zealous, though, and come at me with "kitchen sink" questions—usually numbered—and covering an amazing variety of topics. I can't resist providing my favorite as an example:

Sorry to bother you, but I need to collect information from a few different religions regarding their belief and organization. Would you or someone you may refer help me? I need short answers for some questions (100 words or less) for a project due in 4 weeks. The answers shouldn't be too technical or too profound, just basic.

Thanks in advance for your help.

- *Describe God*
- *Does God appreciate your religion more than others?*
- *How did you arrive to your acceptance of your church?*
- *How did your religion start?*
- *What does your church think about Jesus Christ?*
- *What is the main point(s) of your religion?*
- *What should a person do (if anything) to go to heaven?*
- *What is your church's position on the following:*
- *Baptism*
- *Bible*
- *Creation*
- *Eternal Life*

- *Holy Ghost*
- *Jesus Christ*
- *Marriage*
- *Resurrection*
- *Sin*
- *Do you agree with everything that your church teaches?*
- *Which point(s) do you disagree more strongly?*
- *Who, in your church, can modify general rules or regulations?*
- *What may be your church's major contribution to the world today?*

Just in case you're wondering, I didn't do her homework for her—I referred her to pertinent websites as often as I could and think I may have been at least a little profound once or twice . . . but have you ever tried to describe God in 100 words or less? It's an interesting challenge—the paragraph following this one has 117 words in it.

Not surprisingly, I also spend a great deal of time attempting to explain the difference between Mennonites and the Amish and all the groups in-between. Then there are always those just itching for a good argument—usually regarding homosexuality or pacifism. And now and then I get a question completely out of left field—from the man looking for some "Mennonite sausage," like some he was served in Alberta, to the guy who wanted to join an Amish community because he was pretty sure that there would be no electricity after the rapture, compounding his worry with much talk of the beast and the ten virgins. These are the questions that make for entertaining dinner conversation.

But the ones I really find touching are from the people who are on a true faith journey. I've been surprised by how many letters I've gotten from weary souls looking for a faith which follows the teachings of Jesus who think maybe the Mennonites have what they're looking for. These are the people who make all those explanations about coverings worthwhile. And it's also been a lesson for me that the opportunity to share my faith can occur in the most surprising places. Ten years ago, I never would have guessed that between loads of laundry and fixing kids' snacks I would be directing people to the nearest Mennonite church or debating salvation with someone I've never met, often while wearing pajamas and drinking lukewarm coffee.

I do my best to answer every person as completely and helpfully as I can—even the ones I suspect of pulling my leg (the guy who asked if burning people at the stake is part of our church discipline, for one). And I offer this little book to provide others with insight to the questions people ask about Mennonites. More than the answers I provide, I think the questions themselves highlight the misconceptions and curiosity people have about Mennonites as well as the thinking and spiritual journeys people of today experience.

If it seems that I quote too often from *Confession of Faith in a Mennonite Perspective*, this is also meant to be reassuring: I'm not functioning as a lone ranger but, rather, leaning heavily on accepted statements of the church as we seek to provide responses.

Each question in this book is a genuine question I've received but has been edited for length and grammar (unless the mistakes are deliberate or particularly charming). All names and personal information have been removed to protect privacy.

—*Jodi Nisly Hertzler*
  Harrisonburg, Virginia

Introduction: How Did This Work of Answering Questions About Mennonites Begin?

Third Way Media, and its predecessor organizations Mennonite Media and earlier Mennonite Broadcasts, Inc., has by necessity answered questions from the general public about "Who are Mennonites?" almost from its beginning days. Having a radio program on the air with the name "The Mennonite Hour" starting in 1952 exposed people to the program name. Then when they wrote to the program they frequently misconstrued it as "Midianite Hour," "Man of the Knight Hour," "Moonlight Hour," "Minnow Night Hour" (according to Hubert R. Pellman's early history of the organization *Mennonite Broadcasts: The First 25 Years*).

One can only imagine what went on in the minds of radio listeners when they heard the name *Mennonite*. Mix in massive confusion propagated by the media's continual erroneous references to "Mennonite" when Amish, Old Order, or another group was meant. No wonder that major surveys done in 1989 and 1999 showed forty to sixty percent of people had major confusion about Mennonites.

Thus this organization, which I've been a part of since 1975, has long provided resources—such as the "About the Mennonite Church" brochure series that has probably gone through at least fifteen major revisions since it debuted in the mid-1980s. The pamphlet's current incarnation from Mennonite Church USA is titled "Who are the Mennonites?" Along with such paper resources, we've attempted to provide personal handling of inquiries first by letter, later by 800 number and then e-mail.

Since 1998, we've provided the *Third Way Café* website at www.thirday.com as an online venue for fielding such questions and as a place to publish the most frequently asked questions. Over the years, Mennonite Church USA, Mennonite Publishing House/Network, Mennolink, and occasional other organizations have all forwarded questions they receive of this nature to Third Way Media for handling.

A remarkable list of people, who would have all described themselves as very ordinary Mennonites, have provided this personal answering service for the church. John L. Horst, Moses Slabaugh, Eva Stauffer, Paul Roth, Anna Marie Steckley, David D. Yoder, Marian Bauman, Sheri Hartzler, Minnette Hostetler, Erma Hess Brunk, Ruth Ann Miller Brunk, and currently Jodi Nisly Hertzler are representative of those who've provided this personal voice over the years. All of these correspondents enjoyed it—most of the time—seeing it as unique calling and ministry. They've been helped by their spouses, pastors, seminary professors (and some seminary presidents), retired missionaries (oh yeah, there should be no such thing).

For this book, Jodi was particularly indebted (at least in the beginning) to the files and records of correspondence of her predecessors and especially those kept by Erma Brunk who enjoyed this work from 1997 to 2001 until her too-early death of cancer. I have had the privilege of supervising this work since the mid 1980s, very happy that there have been people to turn to accomplish this time-consuming yet fascinating and rewarding work.

But now Jodi has established her own voice and her own inimitable style of responding that seems to fit our current times well: Her answers are straightforward, direct, informal, caring—yet always on the lookout for the occasional customer who is just out for a fight or pulling our collective leg. Enjoy.

—*Melodie Davis*
   Harrisonburg, Virginia

50 COMMON AND QUIRKY QUESTIONS ABOUT MENNONITES

Chapter One

WHAT DO MENNONITES BELIEVE IN?

1. I had never heard of the term *Mennonites* before but came across it while looking for biblical answers to the question of whether a woman should cover her head in church or not. After viewing your website, I really do not see the difference between "Mennonite" and any other Bible-believing Christian. At my church we do not advocate infant baptism either. So why aren't you called Christians?

Well, first of all, let me make it abundantly clear that Mennonites *are* Christians. The term *Mennonite* classifies us just as other Christian groups are classified "Baptist," "Presbyterian," or "Methodist," for example.

On most counts, Christian churches are more alike than different. As with the rest of the Christian world, Mennonites believe in a loving Creator God; we believe that through the life, death, and resurrection of Jesus Christ, we receive the gift of salvation; we believe that the Holy Spirit empowers the church as individuals and a corporate body to continue Christ's ministry in our world; and we believe in the authority of Scripture.

So what makes Mennonites different? It's key to note that Mennonites greatly emphasize the life and teachings of Jesus Christ and believe we are called to live as his disciples in all things. We therefore subscribe to an ethic of love that rejects violence in all spheres of human life. We believe that peace is a way of life—peace with one's family, church members, neighbors, and all human beings everywhere in the world.

Other distinctives include our practice of believers baptism, the understanding that Scripture is to be interpreted by the community of believers, a strong focus on a separation of church and state, a non-hierarchical structure of the church, emphasis on community, nonconformity in relation to ethics and justice issues, and focus on simple living and stewardship issues.

Again, I realize that even as I call these things "distinctives," there are many churches that share many of these beliefs and practices. Sometimes what ends up making a particular Christian group unique are subtleties—hard to describe in just a few words—created by a combination of beliefs and tradition/culture that create a unique entity.

2. I am doing a project for school, and I have a question. What are the benefits of Anabaptism? What is accomplished by waiting to baptize members?

Well, the benefit is that only people who have deliberately made the choice to be baptized are in fact baptized. The choice to live a Christ-centered life is not an easy one.

It's a major commitment that a person makes to God and to the church family, and it's not to be taken lightly. When an infant is baptized, the sacrament seems to Mennonites to lose some power, as it reflects the parents' beliefs and not the child's. We do practice what we call "infant dedication," a small but meaningful ceremony in which parents dedicate their child to the care of God and the church, so that type of celebration isn't left out, but we reserve baptism for people who can make the choice for themselves and can understand the meaning of what they are doing.

We believe that the baptism of believers with water is a sign of their cleansing from sin. It is also a pledge before the church of a person's covenant with God to walk in the way of Jesus Christ through the power of the Holy Spirit. We believe that Christian baptism is for those who confess their sins, repent, accept Jesus as Lord and Savior, and commit themselves to follow Jesus in obedience as members of his body. These are not things infants can do. We believe the church is strengthened when made up of adults who have made the decision to follow Christ and be baptized and can remember the impact of that ceremony in their Christian walk.

3. In the Catholic Church, we speak of the "age of reason" (when a person may receive Holy Communion) as generally occurring about age seven and the "age of discernment" (when he/she may be confirmed) which occurs during adolescence. What is the age of accountability (when Mennonites may be baptized)?

The age at which a youth may be baptized is a decision made by each congregation, the youth, and the parents. Usually those baptized are at least twelve. In my experience, for kids who grow up in the church, the usual age is closer to sixteen. Most congregations offer some sort of class for persons who are interested in being baptized (usually led by one of the church pastors). The class would include Mennonite history as well as reading and discussion of the *Confession of Faith in a Mennonite Perspective*. The pastor often meets individually with each person so they can decide together if the applicant is ready to be baptized.

4. Could you give me any information on the views of Mennonites of death? I am a hospice worker who is going to work with a Mennonite family, and I have been unable to find information on their beliefs regarding end of life and death.

Mennonites believe that we are created in the image of God; therefore life is precious. We want to make certain that the best care is given to the person who is ill. We believe that God remains with us faithfully through death and that there is eternal life with God after death. Therefore death is not something to be feared. There are no specific death or burial rituals that Mennonites follow, but many aim for funeral practices that honor simplicity in style and cost. The church does not have a formal position on issues such as cremation or organ donation; such decisions are left to the individuals and their families. Memorial services after burial or cremation are common; services focus on celebrating the life of the loved one and on God's faithfulness and the assurance of salvation. Autopsies may take place if requested.

You might want to take a look at our section titled "Facing Death" on the Third Way Café website.

5. I cannot seem to find information on what Mennonites believe in terms of heaven, hell, and the afterlife including purgatory. I would greatly appreciate any information you could give me.

Mennonites do believe in heaven; we believe that at death, the faithful receive the gift of salvation and eternal life in the presence of God.

We don't believe in purgatory, but we do believe in some form of hell, or at least in eternal separation from the presence of God. Most modern Mennonites would hesitate to draw clear lines as to how the final judgment is to take place. We believe that God in grace and goodness will work out our difficult questions about who suffers and who doesn't.

The *Confession of Faith in a Mennonite Perspective* has this to say in the article concerning the reign of God:

> We believe that, just as God raised Jesus from the dead, we also will be raised from the dead. At Christ's glorious coming again for judgment, the dead will come out of their graves—"those who have done good, to the resurrection of life, and those who have done evil, to the resurrection of condemnation." The righteous will rise to eternal life with God, and the unrighteous to hell and separation from God. (90).

6. If you believe there is a heaven and hell, how can a person find out how to make one and miss the other?

I often get questions from people who are fearful of hell and trying to figure out which religious group has the best "recipe" by which to avoid it. I confess I have a rather difficult time relating to these folks, because I personally focus more on how I live my life from day to day than I do on what will happen when it's over. (This is probably the pragmatic farmer philosophy I've inherited.) I picked this specific question because the "make one, miss the other" phrase so humanly captures the essence of this particular quest.

Mennonites do believe in eternal life. To be honest, although we have hope in eternal salvation, Mennonites tend to focus on living our daily lives as Christ's followers—and not worrying about things we can't know. No one knows what heaven and hell really are, or how the end times will come about, but we have assurance that if we are faithful to God and do our best to live as Christ taught, then we will receive the gift of grace and find eternal life with the Lord.

The Confession of Faith in a Mennonite Perspective outlines the "method" (for lack of a better word) by which we receive salvation (I recommend reading the entire article as well as the Scriptures it references, as I'm only quoting a small part): "When we hear the good news of the love of God, the Holy Spirit moves us to accept the gift of salvation. Our response includes yielding to God's grace, placing full trust in God alone, repenting of sin, turning from evil, joining the fellowship of the redeemed, and showing forth the obedience of faith in word and deed" (35).

7. What does your church believe about the creation of the world?

Mennonites believe that God created the world as an expression of love and sovereign freedom. The church does not officially make a direct statement regarding the positions of creationism versus evolution. That's because the Mennonite church puts the focus on God being the ultimate creator, having ultimate control over his creation. For us, creation could never be considered a random event or cosmic accident. Whether one believes this was done in the biblical six days or over a process of millions of years of evolution is a personal choice (and Mennonites will vary on this matter). But all Mennonites believe that the creation is God-centered, God-started, and God-controlled.

8. I assume from what I've seen online so far that Mennonites are not dispensational with regard to eschatology. Is this indeed true?

Sometimes I wonder if people are just trying to stump me. I really do get questions like this—more often than you'd think. This one required some dictionary work before I could answer, even though I have a vague memory of the college class long ago that taught me all these theories. For those of you who don't speak "theologese," eschatology *refers to the study of end times;* dispensationalism *is one theory which divides biblical history and future events into separate periods, or dispensations.*

The Mennonite church does not take an official position on any of the theories involving the end times. Rather, it allows for a variety of opinions concerning the details of how that might come about. Most of us do believe that Christ will personally return to judge the world, raise the dead, and usher in God's kingdom. But we don't spend too much time arguing about how that will happen, in large part because Jesus himself assured us that we won't understand it, or see it coming. In our *Confession of Faith in a Mennonite Perspective* you will find the following statements:

> We place our hope in the reign of God and its fulfillment in the day when Christ will come again in glory to judge the living and the dead. He will gather his church, which is already living under the reign of God. We await God's final victory, the end of this present age of struggle, the resurrection of the dead, and a new heaven and a new earth. There the people of God will reign with Christ in justice, righteousness, and peace for ever and ever. (89)

9. I would like to know where you stand on issues such as eternal security. Do you believe that you can lose your salvation after once becoming saved?

While Mennonites hold tightly to the belief that we are saved through God's powerful gift of grace, we don't subscribe to the "eternal security," or "once saved, always saved" theology. Though we believe we are saved by God's grace and not by our own merits, we also believe that when we live in Christ, we are called to follow in his footsteps and live a life that follows his example.

All members of the church have free will and can separate themselves from the body of Christ and live a life of sin, even if they once were bound to Christ. If that happens, the church will continue to pray for such persons and to seek their restoration into the community of believers and a right relationship with God, but individuals may still choose to forfeit their right to salvation.

10. I think I heard that Anabaptists don't believe in the "flat-book" relationship of the Old and New Testaments. If that's true, how do they talk about how they view the Testaments' relationship to each other?

Mennonites believe that the New Testament is key to the understanding of God and how we gain salvation. To quote from the *Confession of Faith in a Mennonite Perspective*, Mennonites emphasize "the interpretation of Scripture in harmony with Jesus Christ, in the sense that his life, teachings, death, and resurrection are essential to understanding the Bible as a whole" (24). Mennonites view Christ as the culmination and fulfillment of the Old Testament, so we read the Old Testament through a sort of lens, dictated by Christ's life and teachings.

11. Please do you know if the Gifts of Prophecies and the gifts of speaking in tongues are practiced or allowed in the Mennonite/Amish Mennonite movement? Are these considered necessary? Or are they perhaps outdated?

I would like to begin my answer by quoting from the *Confession of Faith in a Mennonite Perspective*:

We believe in the Holy Spirit, the eternal Spirit of God, who dwelled in Jesus Christ, who empowers the church, who is the source of our life in Christ, and who is poured out on those who believe as the guarantee of our redemption and of the redemption of creation. . . . As a dwelling place of the Holy Spirit, the church praises and worships God and brings forth the fruit of the Spirit. By the gifts of the Holy Spirit, all Christians are called to carry out their particular ministries. . . . By the power of the Holy Spirit, the church preaches, teaches, testifies, heals, loves, and suffers, following the example of Jesus its Lord. (17)

In the Mennonite church, the emphasis is on the work of the Holy Spirit in the life of the church rather than on the importance of receiving certain gifts of the Spirit. We believe that gifts are poured out on the church and that those ministries are welcomed.

Some Mennonites have in fact received the gifts of prophecies and tongues; those gifts are recognized and accepted by the church—but such gifts are not considered "higher" or more important than any other gifts of the Spirit.

The Mennonite church also believes that the fruits of the Spirit are important as we live a life of discipleship: love, joy, peace, an even temper, kindness, goodness, faithfulness, gentleness, self-control.

12. I would like to know specifically your views on homosexuality and abortion.

Most Mennonites believe that some persons have a different sexual orientation, although not all agree whether sexual orientation is a choice. The denominational expectation is that a person who has a different orientation will remain celibate. The teaching position of the church is that we understand the Bible to reserve genital intercourse for a husband and wife in marriage. It is our understanding that this teaching rules out premarital, extramarital, and homosexual genital activity.

The church is not unanimous in its response to this issue. Some congregations are open to and supportive of those with different sexual orientation or involved in lifelong monogamous relationships; some are supportive of homosexuals as persons but ask for celibacy; and some feel the Bible gives strict interpretations of teachings about homosexuality. It remains a topic of high-profile debate, and God's guidance continues to be sought by those on all sides of the issue.

Excerpts from "A Call to Affirmation, Confession and Covenant Regarding Human Sexuality," a statement adopted by the Mennonite General Assembly in 1987, say that

> We affirm that sexuality is a good and beautiful gift of God, a gift of identity, and a way of being in the world as male and female.
>
> We confess our fear and repent of our absence of love toward those with a different sexual orientation

and of our lack of understanding for their struggle to find a place in society and in the church.

We covenant with each other to study the Bible together and expand our insight into the biblical teachings related to sexuality. We understand the Bible to teach that genital intercourse is reserved for a man and woman united in marriage. It is our understanding that this teaching precludes premarital, extramarital, and homosexual genital activity. We further understand the Bible to teach the sanctity of the marriage covenant and that any violation of this covenant is sin.

Mennonites generally believe that abortion is wrong. For most, this belief is based on our understanding of peace and justice issues. We believe that violence is wrong and therefore we witness against all forms of violence.

Confession of Faith in a Mennonite Perspective, article 22, states that

Led by the Spirit, and beginning in the church, we witness to all people that violence is not the will of God. We witness against all forms of violence, including war among nations, hostility among races and classes, abuse of women and children, violence between men and women, abortion, and capital punishment. (82)

13. What is the difference between a missional church and a disciple-making church?

This is a great question. Although one could argue they are one and the same, I think there is a difference and that each is vitally important. A missional church is organized around mission—meaning that everything we do in church is, ultimately, about inviting others into the community of disciples. To speak of the "missional" church reflects a perspective that the church is not just about teaching, nurturing, and serving its own, but about reaching out to others in the community and world.

Traditionally, I believe we think of a disciple-making church as one that focuses on all of the aspects of being Christian disciples, which includes growing, serving, and reaching out to others. That is why I said perhaps we can think of them as one and the same.

14. I am seeking the number and names for Mennonite sacraments. I also want your definition of "sacrament." I live in an area with a preponderance of Anabaptist groups. The three largest parishes are Mennonite. I am seeking to learn as much as I can about their faith system. There seem to be variances among them. Some Mennonites think they have seven sacraments but cannot name them. Nor can they provide me with a definition of "sacrament." This included an ordained Mennonite clergyperson.

This question was answered by David A. Shank, retired missionary pastor and teacher, who helps out when I'm feeling out of my depth.

The idea of "sacrament" comes from the doctrinal language of many church traditions—Catholic, Lutheran, Anglican, Presbyterian, etc. Mennonites emerged out of that European church scene and never have comfortably used the word *sacrament*, perhaps because the term may suggest that it is a purveyor of sacred mystery only the sacred, qualified person can promote.

Mennonites have sometimes spoken of their own practices as "symbols" or "ordinances"—meaning those practices taught/ordained by Christ and the apostles and which also "teach" and "order" their common life of faith. Influential Mennonite leaders from 1900 to 1940 used the language of "ordinance" and taught that there were seven "biblical ordinances": baptism on confession of faith; communion (or the Lord's Supper); washing of the saints' feet; the holy kiss; marriage; ordination of elders/bishops, ministers/preachers of the Word, deacons; and anointing with oil for healing.

The current *Confession of Faith in a Mennonite Perspective* refers to "sacrament," "symbol," and "ordinance" but prefers the words of "sign" for baptism and communion; "act" for ordination; "covenant" for marriage; and "parable" for foot-washing.

15. Recently, my family and I have been visiting a Mennonite fellowship and have been richly blessed by the experience. Soon, we will have an opportunity to participate in communion. Please explain the communion emblems to me. Is the bread made with yeast or is it unleavened? Is the wine fermented or is it unfermented grape juice? I don't mean to appear petty, but if the traditions are significantly different than what my family is used to, we want to be mentally prepared to avoid a potentially awkward situation.

You don't sound at all petty. I agree that not knowing what to expect can be off-putting, and it's always better to just ask. There isn't actually a policy that dictates the details of the communion emblems—individual churches are free to decide on the particulars. Mennonites historically abstained from alcohol; so generally, unfermented grape juice is used for communion. There tends to be more variety in the bread that is chosen. I've experienced both leavened and unleavened bread, so I wouldn't be surprised to see either, though in my experience, leavened bread—often homemade—is more commonly used.

You might find it helpful to contact the pastor of the church you are attending and simply ask how that particular congregation generally celebrates communion. I don't think he or she would take any offense in the question—all churches have their own ways of doing things, and it's easy for newcomers to feel awkward at first.

16. Does the Mennonite doctrine teach that it is acceptable to have women preachers and women teaching men?

Although this is not necessarily the case in more conservative Mennonite groups, Mennonite Church USA and Canada have supportive statements about women in leadership and ministry. The most recent *Confession of Faith in a Mennonite Perspective* says that "The church calls, trains, and appoints gifted men and women to a variety of leadership ministries on its behalf. These may include such offices as pastor, deacon, and elder as well as evangelists, missionaries, teachers, conference ministers, and overseers (59)." This understanding of leadership is based on Scriptures in Ephesians 4: 11-13; 1 Corinthians 12:28; Romans 12:6-8; Titus 1:5-9.

This is the ideal toward which much of the Mennonite church strives. Various groups within the Mennonite church are at different places when we discuss women in leadership. In the past, women were not permitted to have a role of leadership ministry. Today some churches will not accept women in these roles. Other churches accept women as worship leaders, song leaders, Sunday school teachers, etc., but not as lead pastors. Others, and the number is increasing, accept women as pastors or in other lead ministry roles. On a denominational level, women have served as moderator and heads of major boards in Mennonite Church USA and Canada.

Chapter Two

WHO STARTED IT?

17. What is the history of the mennoite (sic)? Where/how did it originate?

Anabaptists (a term which means "re-baptizers") grew out of the Protestant Reformation in the early 1500s; the Anabaptist movement began with a group of adults who baptized each other in Zurich, Switzerland. Anabaptists were of the opinion that the church-state had lost the meaning of Jesus' teachings, and urged people to focus on Scripture and the life of Christ as well as the example of the early church. They believed that baptism should be an adult decision and that we are called to lead lives of discipleship. They also believed strongly in a separation between church and state. Because of these radical (for that time) beliefs, Anabaptists endured heavy persecution and were forced to worship and baptize in secret.

Mennonites are one of the groups descended from the Anabaptist movement. They were named after an early Anabaptist leader, theologian, and prolific writer, Menno

Simons. The name *Mennonite* was actually coined by others, but eventually Mennonites adopted the name for themselves. Fleeing persecution, Mennonites spread from Europe to Russia and the Americas. To read further details about our history, you can visit the Third Way Café website and look at the sections titled, "Who are the Mennonites: A Brief History" and "MennoLite."

18. Why do they speak German?

Because the faith started in Switzerland and the Netherlands, many Anabaptists (and later, Mennonites) spoke German and Dutch. Currently, though, there aren't many Mennonites who continue to speak German. In the U.S, there are many conservative Mennonite and Amish groups who speak Pennsylvania Dutch, a German dialect; they use the more formal German in their worship services and often read from German Bibles. There are also some Mennonite churches in Canada and Mexico where German or *Plattdeutsch* (Low German) is still spoken.

19. I would like to know the differences between Mennonite faith and origins and Amish faith and origins. Also, is there a connection to the Quaker faith?

The Mennonites and Amish have common historical roots. Their beginnings (1525) date from a group of persecuted radical Christians nicknamed "Anabaptists" at the time of the Protestant Reformation in Europe. They sought to return to the simplicity of faith and practice as seen in the early Christian church in the Bible. The Amish divided from the Mennonites in 1693. Jacob Amman, a young Swiss Mennonite elder who felt the church was losing its purity, led the group that separated. They were nicknamed "Amish." One of the main areas of debate centered on the "ban" or "shunning" of people who were not living according to the guidelines of the church. The Mennonites believed that if persons changed their way of life, they could be welcomed back into church fellowship. The Amish wanted a stricter ban.

All Amish and Mennonite groups are Christian fellowships and in most cases are still closely related theologically. There is a stress on belief resulting in practice. Emphases on lifestyle, community, and peace have distinguished most of the groups through the centuries. There are obviously differences in specific lifestyle choices, with the Amish and Old Order Mennonite groups stressing the need for separation from the secular world, whereas more modern Mennonite groups tend to express their separation in terms of social consciousness.

As far as I am aware, there is little *historical* connection between the Quaker faith and the Amish/Mennonite faiths, though there certainly are similarities. Quakerism began in England about 100 years after the Anabaptist movement began. Both groups could be considered separatists, freethinkers who struck out against the established church. Both groups were persecuted for their beliefs, and both migrated to the Americas. William Penn, a Quaker, allowed a space for many Mennonites and Amish to live and worship in peace. The Mennonites who in about 1690 founded the first Mennonite congregation in America in Germantown (now part of Philadelphia) had earlier worshipped with Quakers. Both churches are peace churches, and there are certainly other theological similarities.

20. I didn't know much about the history of Mennonites in regards to the history of slavery

and civil rights here in the U.S. I was wondering if you could provide me with information about the Mennonite church's attitudes, policies, and practices in regards to these issues not only today but also in the last hundred years or so.

In 1688, a pamphlet titled *Germantown Protest* was published by Mennonites and Quakers in Pennsylvania. That document was the first public protest against slavery in the U.S. by any group. During the Civil War, some Mennonites were active participants in the Underground Railroad. Margaret H. Rhodes of Virginia is known to have hidden up to six people in a secret place under the floor of her bedroom, and she acted as a "postmaster," delivering messages from escaped slaves to their families and friends.

For centuries, Mennonites avoided overt political activism, preferring to live quiet, peaceful lives while witnessing against war by maintaining conscientious objector status and providing aid to victims of war and other disasters. It wasn't until after World War II that Mennonites became more politically active, such as by protesting nuclear weapons and later, in the 1960s, by participating in the civil rights movement and sometimes protesting the Vietnam War.

Outside the realm of political activism, Mennonites were reaching out to the African-American community long before the civil rights movement, often through Bible schools, church camps, and voluntary service units. From the time the first African-American members were baptized in 1897 to the present, the Mennonite African-American population has continued to grow, and this growth is significantly rooted in the vision and efforts of the first African-American Mennonite bishop, James Lark. (He was ordained pastor in 1945 and bishop in 1954.)

In 1955, as a result of a conference on Christian race relations, a pronouncement, "The Way of Christian Love in Race Relations," was adopted by the Mennonite Church.

That document emphasized the scriptural opposition to discrimination based on race and renewed the church's commitment to actively promote positive actions to overcome society's prejudices.

In 1969, the Mennonite Church adopted a resolution in response to the Black Manifesto, reaffirming the 1955 resolution and stressing the need for outreach to minorities in troubled urban areas as well as the continued need for Mennonite institutions and congregations to be equal opportunity employers. Further resolutions on racism have been adopted in more recent years, and Mennonite Church USA and many of its agencies have active antiracism teams and policies.

The African-American Mennonite Association (AAMA) advocates for African-American and African-American integrated congregations under the Mennonite Church USA umbrella. Currently, there are about fifty-seven AAMA congregations in the U.S. The fastest-growing Mennonite congregation in the country is an African-American congregation in Hampton, Virginia.

21. Are the Mennonites and Mormons living in Colonia Juarez in Casas Grandes, Chihuahua, Mexico one and the same? I grew up in the area and that has always been the case. Is this a unique situation?

I've gotten questions confusing Mennonites and Mormons several times, though never in quite this detail. Usually, it's people wanting to know if Mennonite men can have more than one wife. As the conservative branches of both groups dress in similar ways and live simple, separate lifestyles, (and since both groups have names that start with the letter "M") the confusion is somewhat understandable. But there really are very few similarities.

I'm not an expert on the Mennonite colonies in Mexico, but I'm surprised to hear that in your experience they are associated with Mormons. The two faiths really have little to do with one another, in history or theology, though perhaps these two transplanted, insular communities outwardly seem to have much in common and the names may seem similar to some. I've done some research, and while both groups may appear similar on the surface (dress, simple lifestyle, etc.), I've found nothing other than location to link the two.

Canadian Mennonites began settling in Mexico in 1922 following the granting of a "Privilegium" (privileges) by the Mexican government. In exchange for farming the land and providing the majority of the cheese needed for the northern Mexican region, they were sold land for a low price and permitted to live tax free. In addition, they were given full control of their schools, freedom to speak their own language, freedom of religion, and freedom from military service. While some changes have occurred (for example, their schools are now fully accredited by the Mexican government), they continue to live isolated from the society around them and have received permission from the government to remain so. They continue to speak German (though most now also speak Spanish) and to dress in conservative clothing. Many do live in Chihuahua, as you've experienced, and are called "Old Colony Mennonites."

Mormons, on the other hand, started immigrating to Mexico from the U.S. in 1885, primarily escaping persecution for their practice of plural marriages. Most of those colonies were evacuated during the Mexican Revolution, due to anti-American sentiment. Only a small number eventually returned to their property, and there are only two settlements in Mexico today, the one you mentioned and one in Colonia Dublan.

22. I find myself wanting to learn more about the Mennonite faith. Specifically, what denominations are there? I would like to eventually learn enough so that I can feel comfortable enough to visit a church. Are there any resources on the different Mennonite churches?

It can be somewhat tricky to clearly define different Mennonite groups, as the differences are sometimes fairly minor. We all focus on pacifism, on community, on discipleship, and on stewardship/simple living, for example. But historically, as the Mennonite/Anabaptist church grew and developed, people didn't always agree on how best to live those beliefs or to interpret certain issues in the Bible. Some churches were split by issues that seem quite minor to us today—the use of pulpits in the church, buttons on clothes, whether to have Sunday school.

There are over fifty different groups of Mennonites. If you include Amish, Brethren, and Hutterite groups, the number goes up significantly. Many of those groups include only a handful of churches, and many are so conservative they don't have readily available phone/e-mail information.

Mennonite Church USA is the largest and most modern Mennonite group and shares many historical ties and styles of thinking and functioning with its north-of-the-border counterpart, Mennonite Church Canada. If you include other Anabaptists in your search, the Mennonite Brethren and the Church of the Brethren would be quite compatible in terms of theology, dress, and comfort with technology/modern living. The next largest Mennonite denomination is the Conservative Mennonite Conference. Then you would have the groups that lie somewhere between the Amish and the Mennonites—Beachy Amish, various Old Order groups, New Order Amish, and more.

The book *Anabaptist World USA* by Donald Kraybill and C. Nelson Hostetter has a handy table which explains the difference between different Mennonite groups:

TRADITIONAL GROUPS:
- use horse-drawn transportation
- speak a special dialect
- consider themselves Old Order
- selectively use technology
- preserve older forms of religious ritual
- emphasize traditional practices
- practice nonresistance
- accept the collective authority of the church
- wear plain clothing

TRANSITIONAL GROUPS:
- encourage individual religious experience
- emphasize rational, formal, written doctrine
- engage in evangelism
- use technology except television
- forbid divorce
- forbid the ordination of women
- discourage higher education
- ordain lay pastors
- practice nonresistance
- wear plain clothing

TRANSFORMATIONAL GROUPS:
- support higher education
- engage in diverse forms of ministry
- hold professional jobs
- hire professional, salaried pastors
- widely use forms of technology
- are involved in peacemaking and social justice
- accept individualism
- participate in mainstream cultural activities
- operate large church organizations
- participate in local, state, and national politics (56)

As that summary shows, not all Mennonites actively separate from the world in their day-to-day activities (except in subtle ways) but rather in their spiritual lives. More conservative groups do maintain separation by limiting their exposure to mainstream culture and by placing a stress on tradition and the "Old Order."

Chapter Three

ARE MENNONITES ALLOWED TO FIGHT PEOPLE WHO ATTACK THEM?

Mennonites are well known as pacifists, and as such, I find myself regularly fielding questions on the subject. World events post-September 11, 2001, have brought the issue to a forefront. Many people are drawn to Mennonites because they find themselves at odds with U.S. policy; others are deeply offended at our lack of patriotism.

Whatever the reason, however, I find myself pleased that the discussion is taking place, and even when people are upset or skeptical (that whole "But what if your family were being attacked?" issue), I trust that God is at work in these conversations.

23. Is there freedom regarding the issues of war and capital punishment among the Mennonites? That is, can one believe in both capital punishment and the possibility of just war and be a part of a Mennonite congregation? Your help will be

appreciated. (I am looking for a church home, and many Mennonite emphases fit for me.)

In the *Confession of Faith in a Mennonite Perspective,* the church does make a statement against war and capital punishment:

> As disciples of Christ, we do not prepare for war, or participate in war or military service. The same Spirit that empowered Jesus also empowers us to love enemies, to forgive rather than to seek revenge, to practice right relationships, to rely on the community of faith to settle disputes, and to resist evil without violence.
>
> Led by the Spirit, and beginning in the church, we witness to all people that violence is not the will of God. We witness against all forms of violence, including war among nations, hostility among races and classes, abuse of children and women, violence between men and women, abortion, and capital punishment. (82)

The peace position is a major component of the Mennonite identity, and for some, it becomes the proverbial "line in the sand" that simply cannot be crossed if one wishes to be a member of the Mennonite church. That said, there is sometimes a range of opinions among individuals; I personally know Mennonites who are not opposed to capital punishment or to the government's use of military force in certain situations. So I asked a pastor friend what he counsels persons who might come to him in your position. Here is part of what he said:

> We have tried to work gently with people who don't share our theology. We like to approach it as a journey toward Christ and believe that they are on the way, having not yet arrived at the same position we may have reached as a congregation. Peace is definitely one of those issues. If we feel that people are open to

the peace position and do not oppose us or openly advocate military support and involvement, we invite them to consider membership with us and walk with them in that process, hoping and praying that they will some day endorse the peace position. We feel it is important not to needlessly offend people who worship with us who aren't in agreement with our theology. We certainly want them to know that we welcome their continuing as part of our fellowship even if we don't agree on all faith issues.

24. Would most Mennonites today sing the national anthem, put up a flag, or recite the pledge of allegiance for their country? Would there be any differences in terms of willingness to do these things for a peaceful nation or a nation at war?

Here's what the Confession *of Faith in a Mennonite Perspective* has to say:

We believe that the church is God's "holy nation," called to give full allegiance to Christ its head and to witness to all nations about God's saving love.

The church is the spiritual, social, and political body that gives its allegiance to God alone. As citizens of God's kingdom, we trust in the power of God's love for our defense. The church knows no geographical boundaries and needs no violence for its protection. The only Christian nation is the church of Jesus Christ, made up of people from every tribe and nation, called to witness to God's glory. (85)

Most Mennonites do not sing the national anthem, display a flag, or recite the Pledge of Allegiance. We do respect and pray for our political leaders. We obey laws and most pay taxes. But if we claim to give our allegiance to God *alone*, then we can't pledge allegiance to any national flag or sing the national anthem. Our focus is on being disciples of Christ and enacting God's all-encompassing love in the world. That position would not change whether we were in a state of war or not, in the U.S. or a different country; we would simply continue to pray that God direct the actions of our leaders and that a peaceful resolution might be found. Additionally, in times of war, we seek ways to offer relief and restoration to those whose lives are affected.

Sometimes there are gray areas in which an individual has to make a personal decision—for example, some Mennonites withhold the portion of their taxes that would be directed toward the military; others do not. And while the more modern groups of Mennonites tend to be more open to voting and participating in politics, the more conservative groups generally refrain from any involvement of this sort.

25. I want to know what the church's opinion is on gun ownership. I have two guns that I have never used except for target practice. I do not believe in hunting and would not use them for self defense. They are disassembled and in a gun safe. Is this okay with the Mennonite church?

Also, I began Tae Kwon Do years ago to spend time with my two sons. We are now Black Belts. How does the Mennonite church view Tae Kwon Do?

Both of these issues fall into a gray area and really have to be determined by the individual. The key is whether either the guns or the martial arts are to be used to inflict harm on another person. If the guns are kept merely for target practice, and the martial arts regarded as an exercise/discipline, most Mennonites wouldn't have a problem. Many Mennonites hunt and own hunting rifles, and I don't think that's ever been an significant issue—in fact, a good argument in the spirit of simplicity can be made for hunting to feed one's family as opposed to purchasing meat that has traveled who-knows-how-far to the grocery store. Many Mennonites would be uncomfortable with owning a handgun or any gun not designed for hunting, but that's still considered a personal decision, as long as the gun is only used for target practice.

26. Do Mennonites sit on juries? I have heard that the Amish do not. Is that true? Generally what do you think Mennonites believe about trials?

This is an issue left to an individual to decide. When it comes to things like voting, accepting a public office, or sitting on a jury, each person must decide: "Will this participation in the government or in other institutions of society enable us to be ambassadors of Christ's reconciliation? Or will participation violate our commitment to the way of Christ and compromise our loyalty to Christ?" (These questions are taken from the *Confession of Faith in a Mennonite Perspective*, Article 23.)

It's true that Old Order Mennonites and the Amish do not sit on juries. The majority of individuals in the more modern Mennonite groups would be comfortable with the idea (though our positions on issues like capital punishment might mean we wouldn't actually be selected for the jury). But some Mennonites feel that participating on a jury requires us to judge another person, which goes against the biblical principal, "judge not, that you might not be judged." Or they might have other reservations so would opt out of jury duty (if able to do so legally).

Most modern groups respect and appreciate the justice system, and many Mennonites are practicing lawyers. However, Mennonites are concerned about the growing litigiousness of our society. We are slower to prosecute than the average American citizen, preferring to seek reconciliation and offer forgiveness—such as through victim-offender reconciliation programs—rather than revenge.

For the Amish or Old Order groups, though, there is a resistance to any governmental program, including the police or court system. Generally, the Amish don't report incidents unless a person is hospitalized or killed. The reason for this rationale can be found in Matthew 5:39. There Jesus teaches, "Do not resist an evil person. If someone strikes you on the right cheek, turn to him the other also." Likewise, it is almost unheard-of for a member of the Amish church to sue anyone . . . for any reason.

27. To be consistent with the Mennonite faith, how should one deal with a neighbor when one finds oneself in a dispute? (Whether it is a dispute as the result of an action, or an apparent dispute as the result of having a different philosophy.)

The Mennonite Church adopted a resolution on this topic in 1995 titled, "Agreeing and Disagreeing in Love." To summarize that statement: We are to pray about the situation first, and then go to the other person in a spirit of openness and humility. When we speak, we are to be quick to listen and slow to judge, always willing to negotiate or accept mediation from objective parties. If a resolution cannot be reached one-on-one, the adversaries must then trust the community of believers to decide what should happen and then accept that decision.

This is not to say that we are always successful at following this prescribed course of action, but we do emphasize mediation, negotiation, and working things out privately or within the community. Mennonites have been strongly involved in the conflict mediation initiatives in many communities across the U.S. and Canada.

28. What passage of the Bible would refer to a Mennonite's lack of political interest and especially those who do not exercise their right to vote? About what percentage of Mennonites does not register to vote or actually go to the voting polls? We have made friends with a Mennonite couple who do not vote—yet they do not know why.

The decision whether to vote is a personal one, and individual Mennonites may have different reasons for not voting. If your friends don't know why they don't vote, it's probably because historically Mennonites stayed out of government affairs and felt that voting would compromise the separation between church and state. Many Mennonite communities and individuals today continue that pattern.

There are a number of reasons Mennonites might choose not to vote. One is the concern that we are to be in the world without belonging to the world. Another is our peace position—one arm of every government is military, and many Mennonites feel that to be involved in any government process is to compromise our pacifist stance.

That said, there has been a shift in more recent history toward involvement in politics and the political process. We often disagree with the actions and decisions made by our leaders, but many Mennonites also feel that we need to give voice to an alternative way of thinking and we need to encourage our leaders to consider nonviolent solutions to world and civil problems.

A profile of Mennonite Church USA members was conducted in 1996. (Results can be found in Conrad Kanagy's *Roadsigns for the Journey*.) Kanagy reports that 93 percent of respondents said that they believe it is important for Mennonites to vote. That's up from 66 percent in 1972 (124). I corresponded with the General Secretary of the Conservative Mennonite Conference, who didn't know exact numbers, but estimated that 75 percent of their members vote.

So trends are changing, but there would still be a strong contingent of Old Order groups and individuals across the Mennonite spectrum who feel that we aren't to involve ourselves in worldly agendas.

29. Assuming a completely passive response to violence (or rather answering violence with positive action and faith), if I was a centerline Mennonite, would I have the church's blessing to call for law enforcement assistance if there was a stranger in my house committing serious violence against my family? If I would not have their blessing to call for aid, how would the church teach me to care for my family during such a situation? If I would have their blessing, the cop (who has a gun) would not likely maintain a passive response regarding the stranger in my home. Would that not be a violence response by proxy?

What would the church expect a typical Mennonite man/father to do if, while at the park with his family, a stranger picked up his child and began to flee (attempting a kidnapping)?

These issues are definitely gray areas, and individuals within the Mennonite church find themselves at different points on the spectrum. It's certainly a conundrum. Many of us would call the police if we felt ourselves or our families threatened. But there has certainly been discussion about whether such a response implies tacit approval of possible violence on the police's part. I've heard those who oppose the idea of calling the police say that they would attempt to restrain someone intent on causing harm to another (if escape were impossible) or that they would draw the violence to themselves but would not go so far as to hurt or kill the perpetrator, no matter what.

I don't think any Mennonite parents would just stand still and watch someone make off with their child. We wouldn't necessarily wish deadly harm to come to any violent offender, but we don't feel that we need to sit passively by and allow violence to happen, either—that's not loving either the offender or the victim.

I think your first sentence partly answers the question. We are not called to be passive. Jesus certainly wasn't a passive person. But his every action was dictated by love—love for enemies as well as friends. And he asked us to do the same. We are called to answer violence with love and forgiveness, with positive action as opposed to revenge and retaliation. This does not lay out the issue in starkly either/or terms; rather, it is up to individuals to decide how to implant these beliefs into our daily lives and the situations we may face.

Chapter Four

WHY DO THEY
LIVE THE WAY THEY DO?

Here we go: what I think of as the "coverings" questions. People are fascinated with Mennonites in large part because the Old Order groups are so, well, unique. They stand out and inspire curiosity. Most of us who are ethnic Mennonites are accustomed to many of these questions when people learn of our background, so I had a fair amount of practice before starting this job. What these questions have brought to the forefront of my mind is the debate of whether the "modern" Mennonite church is slowly losing its identity as it assimilates more and more of the culture we live in. Can we embrace the comforts modern life has to offer without compromising what makes us unique?

30. As a nun I have taken vows of poverty, chastity and obedience. What do the Mennonites believe about Matthew 19:16-30, and how do they fulfill this in their lives? To me, forsaking the comforts of this world and the amassing of wealth (especially the ties that bind the heart of

those striving to love God when it comes to riches and which seem to cause many people to sin) are crucial.

The Scripture this woman references is the story of the rich young man who asks Jesus how to obtain eternal life. Jesus' response is that he should sell everything he has and give to the poor. When the man goes away in a huff, Jesus comments to his disciples that it is very hard for a rich man to enter the kingdom of heaven.

You ask an excellent question, one Mennonites have long struggled with. I think I would be safe saying that one of the unique aspects of the Mennonite faith is the call to live simple lives. The problem, of course, is in the definition of "simple," as well as the continual influence of the excesses of popular culture. The Amish and Old Order Mennonites have separated themselves from society almost completely and have managed to maintain very simple, humble lifestyles. For us more modern Mennonites, there is a constant struggle to maintain a balance by which we take part in society and yet hold ourselves to a different standard.

Article 21 of the *Confession of Faith in a Mennonite Perspective* discusses Christian Stewardship:

As stewards of money and possessions, we are to live simply, practice mutual aid within the church, uphold economic justice, and give generously and cheerfully. As persons dependent on God's providence, we are not to be anxious about the necessities of life, but to seek first the kingdom of God We cannot be true servants of God and let our lives be ruled by desire for wealth. (78)

This only scratches at the surface of the issue. Individuals have to decide for themselves how to live a simple life, and each church group has to work together to make decisions that affect the entire church body as well as the surrounding community. Like most other groups, Mennonites run the gamut from the extremely wealthy to those who spend their lives in service in developing countries. It is, therefore, hard to analyze how contemporary Mennonites fulfill the direction in Matthew in their lives, but it is an on-going topic of discussion and personal as well as congregational reflection.

31. How do Mennonites dress on a daily basis?

Depends who you're talking about. There are many different Mennonite groups and the guidelines for what women wear varies greatly according to which group of Mennonites you are referring to. For more modern Mennonites, dress is not an issue and is not dictated by leaders. We are simply encouraged to dress modestly. As you can imagine, modesty is subject to interpretation. Women wear slacks, jeans, and shorts as well as skirts and dresses. Women wear a variety of hairstyles, makeup, and jewelry. Men also wear clothes in keeping with popular culture. You would never know most of us are Mennonites if you passed us on the street.

On the other end of the spectrum, the Amish have very distinct guidelines for clothing. Most Amish men wear dark suit coats which have no lapels and fasten with hooks and eyes. Pants are made in an old style, with a flap in front rather than a zipper, and are usually held up by suspenders. Shirts are made of solid-colored fabric. Dress-up shoes are black but work shoes are often brown. Broad-brimmed hats made of either straw or black felt are worn outdoors. Hair is blunt cut and combed front in bangs. Long beards are the mark of an adult man but mustaches are not worn.

Women and girls wear dresses with full skirts made of solid-colored fabric, frequently green, blue, brown, gray, purple and, for some occasions, black. An apron is nearly always worn. A cape, which is like a fitted second bodice over the dress, often covers the bodice of the dress. Black shoes and stockings are proper for going out. The women and girls do not cut their hair. They wear it parted in the middle, combed back from the face, and then twisted in a bun at the nape of the neck. A white, or in some cases black, cap-type head covering is worn in obedience to Scripture in 1 Corinthians 11.

And then many, many groups fall somewhere in the middle. In most of the more conservative groups, women are expected to wear skirts/dresses and coverings. But styles vary considerably according to the tradition and preferences of each group. The less conservative the group, the more mainstream the clothing.

32. I recently was on a cruise and saw a Mennonite group. I noticed that some women wore black scarves, some wore white scarves, and some wore little white net cups over their hair buns. I was curious what the different hair coverings meant. I thought it might mean which ones were single.

For the most part, different types of coverings don't have any "meaning" other than being a reflection of a certain group's preferences or sometimes even an individual's personal tastes. Usually, the style is dictated by leaders of an individual congregation or group, and the decision is made as much by tradition or cultural background as anything else.

Generally, the more conservative the group, the larger, darker, and more bonnet-like the covering. Age can play a minor role in that women begin to wear coverings when they are baptized, and often the younger women in a congregation gravitate toward less conspicuous coverings or scarves. Marital status is likewise not a factor, though if a woman married someone in a different congregation, she would likely adopt the preferred style of her new church family.

33. I assume women wore head coverings because it was scriptural. What is the justification for *not* wearing them now?

Yes, it's true that there is some scriptural defense for wearing a covering—1 Corinthians 11 says, "every woman who prays or prophesies with her head uncovered dishonors her head," and as we are instructed to "pray continually" (1 Thess. 5:17), it was understood that women should have their hair covered at all times. Amish and conservative Mennonite groups continue to wear coverings, but most modern Mennonite women do not. This has more to do with interpretation of Scripture, taking into account the culture in which it was written.

At www.Gameo.org there is an online encyclopedia called *GAMEO* (Global Anabaptist Mennonite Encyclopedia Online), which has an entry on the "Prayer Veil" and goes into some detail about the history of that Mennonite tradition. The last paragraph summarizes the reasons the cultural trend changed for many groups:

> The change of the past generation was largely a response to societal trends and pressures, two of which deserve mention. One was the impact of the feminist movement, which was partly responsible for the ending in 1969 of the nearly 1900-year-old practice of the Roman Catholic Church, which had required women to cover their heads in church. Another factor was the shift in the interpretation of 1 Corinthians 11:2-16. From being understood and taught as an ordinance to be practiced literally by Christian women, the passage is viewed as teaching a principle, but having

been a cultural accommodation to the Corinthian church, and not a binding practice for all times.

34. Do Mennonites have ordained pastors? Do Mennonites ordain women?

Mennonites generally do have ordained pastors. The more conservative and Old Order groups ordain lay pastors, often selecting a member within their church. These pastors seldom have seminary degrees and often have jobs beyond their church work. Although historically the Old Order pattern was common among many Mennonite groups, today the more modern Mennonite churches hire professional, salaried pastors, accepting applications from potential pastors (most often persons who have a seminary degree). Next typically a search committee interviews and selects the applicant(s) seen as best fitting the needs of the church. Then the full congregation affirms a candidate by majority vote or consensus.

Women do not take leadership roles in conservative and Old Order Mennonite churches; however, the modern Mennonite church does ordain women as pastors (though it must be noted that some churches are more open to women in leadership than others; see more, question 16).

35. What holidays do Mennonites celebrate? And if you don't celebrate some of them, why not?

Christmas and Easter are considered our most important holidays, as they are the primary Christian holidays and a time to focus both on what we believe and on our families and communities. Different groups of Mennonites may celebrate differently. For example, the more traditional, conservative groups do not have Christmas trees or use decorations around the house. They may attend a church service on Christmas day. Gifts for the family are usually quite simple.

The more modern groups often enjoy decorations and give more elaborate gifts, though some retain considerable concern about maintaining a spirit of simplicity and avoiding the pervasive commercialism and consumerism of our culture. There often is an emphasis on service projects and giving gifts to the needy as well. For all groups, it is an important family day when large family gatherings are held and good food is enjoyed.

Easter celebrations focus on a worship service, singing, and time for family/church gatherings. Distinctions between styles of celebration are similar to those involving Christmas. More conservative groups would probably not embrace the more "modern" traditions of Easter baskets, decorating eggs, or other practices seen as pagan. Churches often hold evening services on Maundy Thursday or Good Friday, as well, often having communion and/or a foot-washing service as part of that observation.

Many congregations also observe Advent and Lent and center church services around those themes. This tends to be less common among more conservative groups.

We also enjoy Thanksgiving as a time to appreciate the gifts God has provided us. We celebrate in much the same way as most people do, focusing on friends and family— and too much fattening food!

In relation to secular holidays, you'd find some variation depending on how conservative the Mennonite group is. National holidays such as the Fourth of July, Veterans Day, and Memorial Day tend to be dowplayed or ignored by more conservative groups, as those holidays are patriotic and celebrate war efforts and military history. More modern Mennonites might enjoy those days off work as an opportunity to spend with family and friends, but we still will typically not focus on the patriotic history.

Most conservative groups do not celebrate Halloween because of its strong roots in paganism and because they consider it a foolish and "worldly" activity. More modern Mennonite families have a mixed reaction. Some do allow children to dress up and go trick-or-treating; others ignore it altogether because of the history of that holiday. Many have alternative harvest parties or All Saints Day parties the next day instead.

You'll find a similar trend in regard to other holidays (New Year's, Valentine's Day, etc.). Mennonites do try to minimize the secular materialism that seems to have permeated so many holidays, thus many times our decorations or gifts tend to be simpler. But we do enjoy celebrations and time to spend with our families and friends.

36. A colleague's mother died recently. His family follows the Mennonite religion. I wanted to send flowers to the funeral home but am unsure if this is appropriate given that your website indicates funerals are typically simple. I do not want to offend him and his family. I thought an alternative would be to have a rosary of roses—it's basically rosary beads in the form of roses—but I don't know if Mennonites use rosary beads or if this is also inappropriate. I was wondering if you could provide some guidance.

For most Mennonites, a gift of flowers would be considered appropriate at funerals, though some of the more conservative groups wouldn't have flowers in the church. If your colleague and his family aren't obviously very conservative, I think you'd be safe sending flowers—I wouldn't make them too elaborate, but a nice arrangement or plant would most likely be fine. (If it's helpful, all of my grandparents were conservative Mennonites—my grandmothers wore cape dresses and coverings—and there were flowers at their funerals. Probably less ornate than at some, but there were definitely flowers there.) If you have any doubt, though, I would contact the funeral director and ask if the family has any preferences regarding flowers.

Mennonites don't use rosary beads, so that idea probably wouldn't work. If nothing else, cards are always appreciated, even by the most conservative groups.

37. We have a Mennonite friend who is getting married in the spring. Is it acceptable to give the couple a gift? If so, what type of gift is acceptable?

I'm assuming that because you are asking the question your friend is fairly conservative. A wedding gift is certainly appropriate—even in Amish communities, gifts are given at weddings.

A good rule of thumb in determining what to give: The more conservative the group, the more practical/useful the gift should be. It's always safe to give linens (bed, bath, or kitchen) or kitchen/cooking items. Nice serving bowls or platters would also be fine (my grandparents were all very conservative, and various glass and crystal serving dishes have been handed down to me). You can't go wrong with Tupperware, knives, useful kitchen gadgets, or cookbooks. An attractive mantel clock or small table lamp would probably be fine, if you want to give something a little less "useful." One of my favorite wedding gifts was a year-long pass to a nearby national park, presented inside a picnic basket—something similar would be fun and creative but still not frivolous.

38. A few non-Mennonite families recently attended a funeral service for a young married Mennonite man. As we sat waiting for our turn to show our respects, we noticed that as some Mennonite men greeted each other, they kissed each other, not just on the cheeks, but on the lips. While we are quite aware of some of the Mennonite traditions, all of us were somewhat taken aback. We would like some clarification or information about this tradition or significance of the greeting that was taking place.

The history of the "holy kiss" originates in the New Testament, where in four different letters from Paul to different churches, the early Christians are instructed to "greet one another with a holy kiss" (Rom. 16:16, 1 Cor. 16:20, 2 Cor. 13:12, 1 Thess. 5:26). Some churches (not all necessarily Mennonite) take these passages to heart and greet one another with a kiss (on lips or cheek, depending on the group), much as anyone else would greet another person with a hug or handshake. This tends to occur in the more conservative churches and was more prevalent in the past. In the conservative Mennonite and Amish churches where this practice continues, it is strictly understood that the holy kiss is shared only between persons of the same sex.

Most modern Mennonites read these passages in a cultural context. While we still greet one another warmly and offer blessings to one another in various ways, we usually don't actually kiss.

39. Could you tell me a little bit about the culture of birth among Mennonites? Pregnancy behaviors, beliefs, labor, birth, postpartum, newborn cultures?

The church treasures children and considers the birth process to be a powerful and God-present thing—and most Mennonite women who have undergone labor and childbirth would maintain that it's very much a highly spiritual process.

Modern Mennonites are not very different from the general public when it comes to health care; for example, pregnant women generally follow the approved regimen for pre- and postnatal care under the services of a doctor or midwife. Many may choose to refuse tests/screenings to determine any problems in the unborn child. Most give birth in a hospital or birthing center, though some do opt for home births. I would guess that the percentages of women who opt for pain relievers and other procedures during birth and those who choose an intervention-free birth would be similar to that of the general public.

The Amish and more conservative Mennonites are generally more likely to seek a home birth or give birth in a birthing center. Because of a concern for costs, they often prefer to see midwives and avoid any high-tech tests or interventions. In low-risk pregnancies, it is common for these women to reduce the number of prenatal visits to every eight weeks instead of every four. Herbal and other non-traditional remedies are often employed.

The Amish vary in terms of immunizing their children; for the most part, they aren't specifically against the practice but might opt out for financial reasons. Most of the more modern Mennonites do go to doctors for well-baby visits and follow the immunization schedule recommended by the American Association of Pediatrics.

Breastfeeding is encouraged among Mennonite women because of the importance to the newborn. The practice is almost universal among the Amish. However, it is recognized that not all women are able to breastfeed, so there is no stigma placed on the woman who opts not to breastfeed.

The choice to circumcise or not varies according to the preferences of parents.

The church strives to be very supportive of new parents and usually hosts a baby shower before the birth. After the baby is born, we have a blessing ceremony where the child is dedicated to the church, and the church responds by affirming its commitment to support the new family and help raise the child into a Christian life.

40. I am doing a project for school and am interested in the Mennonites' church service. I was wondering if you could tell me the process of your service, i.e.: first prayer, then . . . , then . . . , etc. And if they are a set order of events or spontaneous and any specific items that are religion specific that are always part of the decor.

There really is no mandated order for Mennonite services—they do not follow a prescribed liturgy. Most churches have a worship team/committee which plans what happens on a given Sunday, and while certain elements are almost always present, there's a fair amount of room for variety. Often there is a time of worship led by a worship leader. That time is spent in singing, reading Scripture, and prayer. It frequently includes a children's time and responsive readings, or there might be special music or a drama that pertains to the theme of the service.

After the worship time, a pastor (most likely), church member, or guest speaker gives a sermon, followed by a prayer and/or a song. At some point during the service, there is a time of sharing, responsive prayer, receiving the offering, and announcements. The end of the service is marked by a benediction, either a song or a Scripture.

Mennonites have strong feelings about stewardship, so the decor tends to be simpler than in other churches, though again, this varies by group and by congregation. There is usually a podium in the front, and often a table which might have a plant or flower arrangement on it. There might be banners, artwork, or a simple wooden cross on the walls; there might be other plants/indoor trees at different locations. On special occasions, especially Christmas and Easter (or during the seasons of Advent and Lent), there tends to be more attention paid to decorating and celebration—with flowers, candles, greenery, etc.

41. I have neighbors that are Mennonites. They love to slaughter animals, which I can see if for food, but why do they kill them in such a cruel way? For instance, when they kill chickens, they hang them by their feet before they kill them. They have no feelings for any animal and are taught this from the time they are small. Doesn't the Bible say, "Be kind to your beast?"

Every year we receive at least a couple questions on the subject of animal cruelty, most often about puppy mills. Of all the questions I get, these are the ones I dread most because they are so difficult to really answer satisfactorily.

While it's true that Mennonites feel that we are called to be stewards of the earth—to use and protect it as well as we can—there are a variety of ways to interpret that calling. I couldn't find a Scripture reference which specifically instructs us to be kind to animals, though most people (Mennonites included) feel that it is important to do so. Mennonites believe that God created the world out of love and, in Genesis 1 and 2, gave humans (who were created in his image) dominion over it and the charge to work it; therefore, as God's earthly representatives, we are called to love and take care of creation as God would. The issue here is that not everyone agrees as to how that should happen.

To be honest, I have no idea what the most humane way to kill a chicken would be. But I do know that the more conservative Mennonites tend to view their work on the farm in a very matter-of-fact way, and many may do things in whatever way they find most efficient. I'm not defending some of the practices this may lead to, simply trying to offer a possible explanation. I'm sorry that your neighbors' treatment of their animals upsets you, but I do hope you won't judge all Mennonites by what you perceive as cruelty.

42. Who is the leader of the church? Like the Pope is the leader for Catholics, who is the leader for Mennonites? Or if you don't have a leader, who leads the services?

The Mennonite church is non-hierarchical. This means that we don't have a structure of leadership similar to the Catholic Church, where there is a series of leaders who report to higher-ups until you reach an ultimate authority. Mennonite church structures have upheld the centrality of the church as a community of believers. We believe that the church of Jesus Christ is one body with many members, ordered in such a way that, through the Spirit, believers may be built together spiritually into a dwelling place of God.

In the Mennonite church as in many denominations, decisions are often clarified by majority vote, but an effort is also made to process decisions in such a way as to generate consensus, with each congregation or denominational body seeking the unity of the Spirit. The church aims to listen carefully to all voices, majority and minority. Consensus does not necessarily mean complete unanimity but is reached when the deliberating church body has come to one mind on the matter, or when those who dissent have indicated that they do not wish to stand in the way of a group decision.

Most congregations have a pastor (or pastoral team) who leads services, provides guidance, and helps to care for the members of the church; pastors are supported by various committees, and major decisions are rarely (if ever) made by the pastor alone. In the bigger scope, churches are organized into a variety of assemblies which meet regularly, including local congregations and larger conferences. The local church seeks the counsel of the wider church in important matters relating the faith and life, and they work together in their common mission.

Decisions made at larger assemblies and conferences are confirmed by constituent groups, and local ministries are encouraged and supported by the wider gatherings. Authority and responsibility are delegated by common and voluntary agreement so that the churches hold each other accountable to Christ and to one another on all levels of church life.

43. Are Mennonites allowed to get married?

Yes.

Chapter Five

WOULD IT BE OKAY IF I BECAME A MENNONITE?

It may seem strange to have a whole section for this topic, but you'd be surprised at how many people write to learn how they might become Mennonite (or Amish) . . . or to find out whether some aspect of their lives or their past exempts them from that possibility.

44. I'm a sixteen-year-old, in Brunei. I just really wanted to know where I can find the laws on converting to a Mennonite (if there are any). I'm currently a Muslim, and I just don't feel any connection with that religion whatsoever. My best friend is a Mennonite, and he taught me a lot of his views on God and surprisingly I was really interested. I would like to convert because I don't see any point staying a Muslim when I very obviously don't believe in the religion, and haven't for a long time now. Any help?

We respect whatever ways God chooses to work through Muslim or other religions even as we believe that church membership is for persons who have accepted God's offer of salvation through faith in Jesus Christ. To become a Mennonite you would want to attend a Mennonite church to learn more about our teachings, to have a time of instruction with the ministerial team, and then become part of the church by stating your agreement with our *Confession of Faith* and being baptized. If there are no Mennonite churches in your area, you could certainly identify yourself as being in agreement with the teachings of the Mennonite church.

You've obviously been thinking about this for a while. I would encourage you to continue to do so and also to educate yourself as much as possible about the Mennonite church and our beliefs to make sure this is a step you want to take. I would spend some time reading through the Third Way Café website. The "Who Are the Mennonites" section would be very helpful to you, I think. You should also read the *Confession of Faith in a Mennonite Perspective*, which can be found in its entirety online.

45. Hello—Could you please advise me on a family in an Amish/Mennonite community with whom I might establish a mentorship and move into the community? I wish to convert and raise my child within an Amish/Mennonite community. Any information would be greatly appreciated.

I am part of the modern branch of Mennonites, which is similar in some ways to the Amish and more conservative Mennonite groups (we share the same history and most theological beliefs), but differs in terms of lifestyle and social/political issues.

If you are serious about joining an Amish church, I can't really help you. You'd have to contact someone who is part of the Amish community and discuss the matter with them. The actual transition would depend on the requirements of that particular group, but at the very least it would require living within a community and adopting the lifestyle and belief system. The transition would be difficult, particularly for those of us who are accustomed to living with current technology, and could take years.

The process for joining an Old Order Mennonite church would be similar. But more modern Mennonite groups do not have such stringent lifestyle expectations, and it's easier to join them. Again, you would need to attend a congregation for a time before beginning any sort of membership process. Leaders within the congregation can walk you through that process once you're ready to make a commitment to that church.

46. I have had a long-time interest in the Mennonite and the Amish culture. I am a Baptist, and I was raised Catholic. I was always encouraged to find the answers from God directly from his word. The problem I have is I live in Connecticut, and my husband is military, which I understand is against your religion if I am correct. I also served in the Army as a medic in an emergency room for two years. Are there ever exceptions where the children and the wife can join without the husband?

You bring up some tricky issues, and I'll do my best to help. I think that most Mennonite Church USA-affiliated churches would be open to your family attending and would be willing at least to discuss your membership as well. More conservative churches would have issues with your husband's career and your military history. They might not be open to accepting you as members. While the pacifist stance is still a critical one to the more modern churches, there tends to be more receptiveness, a little more discussion. I won't say there isn't some concern and a feeling of a conflict of interests, but the doors are certainly open, and there's a willingness to dialogue (see more, question 23).

I do know of situations in which one spouse and the children are members while the other remains uninterested. It's certainly not ideal, but it happens. Again, you'll find more openness to this sort of situations in the less conservative congregations.

47. In much of what I have read about [Mennonite] doctrines and practices, I see a heavy emphasis on the divorce and remarriage issue. While I agree that it is unscriptural, I also know that there are people, myself included, who have been divorced and have remarried. So, I have gotten the feeling that I would not be welcome in a Mennonite community because of this action.

The handling of divorce and remarriage tends to vary within the more modern Mennonite churches. While conservative groups do feel strongly that a member cannot divorce and remarry, more modern groups choose to focus on forgiveness and healing. All Mennonites do feel that the marriage relationship is a sacred covenant and not one to be made casually. And we believe that the church is called to support marriages and families and help them through difficult times.

But more modern churches tend to be more open to accepting as members persons who have been divorced and remarried. The *Confession of Faith in a Mennonite Perspective* states that

> Some in the church experience divorce, abuse, sexual misconduct, and other problems that make marriage and family life burdensome or even impossible. Jesus affirmed the sanctity of marriage (Matt. 5:32) and pointed to hardness of the heart as the ultimate cause of divorce (Mark 10:4-9). Today's church needs to uphold the permanency of marriage and help couples in conflict move toward reconciliation. At the same time, the church, as a reconciling and forgiving community, offers healing and new beginnings. The church is to bring strength and healing to individuals and families. (74)

48. Hello, I have been reading and learning a lot about Mennonites. I am very intrigued. I do, however, have a couple of not so common questions: 1.) Is interracial marriage frowned upon? 2.) Will an all-white congregation accept families of mixed races? I know the proper answers to these questions, I just really want the realistic truth.

Interracial marriage is generally accepted by the Mennonite church, as are families of mixed races. In fact, there has been a steady and exciting increase of minorities in U.S. Mennonite congregations in recent years. The make-up of the Mennonite church all over the world is changing rapidly . . . we are no longer a majority of white, European descendants.

A formal statement regarding racism, titled "A Church of Many Peoples Confronts Racism," was created in 1989. Here is an excerpt:

> Racism is a particular social reality of evil our Lord asks us to confront in becoming God's people. . . . The foundation for our concerns is that we have become one in the blood of the crucified Christ (Eph. 2:14), and our membership is to be drawn from every race and tribe and language and nation (Rev. 5:9-10). Our public witness to this fact is an essential part of our evangelism. As representatives of Mennonite congregations throughout North America, we declare here and now that expressions and attitudes of racism are sin and are never acceptable in our Christian life. They must also not be accepted in silence in any of our personal, work, or leisure relationships.

The issue is also addressed in our *Confession of Faith*, which states, "We witness against all forms of violence, including war among nations, hostility among races and classes, abuse of children and women, violence between men and women. . ." (82).

49. My Great, Great, Great Grandfather was L. H. (18__-18__). He was a Minister with the Mennonites in 18__ in Virginia, then in 18__ he moved to Iowa. I am trying to get a little more information on him and also his wife, S.A.T. (18__-19__) I do not know much more than this. Where did L. come from before he was in Virginia or was he born there? I don't know if there are any records your church might have or if you could guide me in the right direction.

I include this question simply as representative of the many genealogical questions we receive. As I have no expertise or resources in genealogical research, all I can do is refer people to someone else who can hopefully help them.

Unfortunately, we do not have access to genealogical resources here, but I can give you some contacts that will hopefully be able to help you:

- MennObits (an index of obituaries from Mennonite periodicals dating back to 1864): *www.mcusa-archives.org/MennObits/index.html*
- Mennonite Historical Library, Goshen College: *www.goshen.edu/mhl/home*
- Mennonite Church USA Historical Committee: *www.mcusa-archives.org/Genealogy/Genealogy Index.html*
- Menno.rec.roots (an online discussion forum for those interested in Mennonite genealogy): *www.mennolink.org/email/reg.cgi?grp+menno.rec.roots*

50. First, I know nothing of your faith. As a Christian I am searching for some answers that I've been missing in my heart and mind. I need a good church home . . . my batteries need recharging. I found your site through an article in *Guideposts*. One of your brethren is a contributing author. Things sounded good until I got into some of your letters from readers. I have to say, the first one online was about some man that hates your church, etc. He is a very bitter soul. I only know what I read in his letters and what a couple of others responded to him.

I had looked up the addresses for your churches close to where I live, but now I don't know if I would be welcome there, not having been born into one of your groups, villages, or whatever they are called. Are you a closed religion? Are you a religion or a way of life as the hippies were in the 1960s?

I honestly do not mean to be rude, but I have no idea what to think and am sort of scared. I read some of your other sites and was so excited to read of your ways and beliefs, should I look any further?

PLEASE answer. I am sincere in my desire to keep my faith in God alive with a group of brethren who follow His words.

I know the above question is longer than most I've included, but I wanted to retain the clear sense of yearning and frustration that this woman was feeling. It was also an excellent reminder to me about not getting too exclusive in my Mennonite identity and to be more considerate of newcomers and their experience. This woman did end up visiting a Mennonite church, and wrote me the kindest thank you letter I've ever received.

I'm not sure which article or responses you are referring to, but it probably doesn't matter. I think there are always going to be people who have bad experiences with any religious group, and that kind of bitterness can remain a long time. So I wouldn't make too many assumptions based on one angry letter.

In truth, I'm sure that there are some fairly exclusive Mennonite churches out there, particularly in the more conservative groups. Conservative Mennonites are much less interested in outreach or community involvement, and there's more suspicion of persons who aren't ethnically Mennonite. If you look at more modern groups, however, I think you'd find quite a contrast in that respect. Churches are growing, and more and more members are joining from all sorts of ethnic and racial backgrounds.

This influx of "new blood" is steadily changing the face of Mennonites and continually adding new traditions and understandings to the mix. To be fair, I think sometimes persons who aren't ethnically Mennonite still feel frustrated by not knowing certain traditions or cultural preferences (have you ever tried shoofly pie? Sung hymn #606?), but there's a growing awareness of this issue, and I think a real effort is being made to broaden our image of who Mennonites are, and to be more welcoming to newcomers.

I would strongly encourage you to visit a church and just see what you think.

REFERENCES

"A Call to Affirmation, Confession and Covenant Regarding Human Sexuality." Mennonite Church. 8 July 1987. Retrieved 21 February 2009. <www.mcusa-archives.org/library/resolutions/humansexuality.html>

"A Church of Many Peoples Confronts Racism." Mennonite Church USA. 3 August 1989. Retrieved 21 February 2009. <www.mcusa-archives.org/library/resolutions/racism.html>

"Agreeing and Disagreeing in Love." Mennonite Church USA. July 1995. Retrieved 23 March 2009. <www.mcusa-archives.org/library/resolutions/agreeing-1995.html>

"Black Manifesto." Mennonite Church. August 1969. Retrieved 23 March 2009. <www.mcusa-archives.org/library/resolutions/BlackManifesto1969.html>

Confession of Faith in a Mennonite Perspective. Scottdale, Pa.: Herald Press, 1995. (Entire text can also be accessed online at <www.mennolink.org/doc/cof/>.)

Kanagy, Conrad L. *Road Signs for the Journey: A Profile of Mennonite Church USA*. Scottdale, Pa.: Herald Press, 2007.

Kraybill, Donald B. and C. Nelson Hostetter. *Anabaptist World USA*. Scottdale, Pa.: Herald Press, 2001.

Mennonite Church. "The Way of Christian Love in Race Relations (Mennonite Church, 1955)." *Global Anabaptist Mennonite Encyclopedia Online*. 1955. Global Anabaptist Mennonite Encyclopedia Online. Retrieved 24 March 2009 <www.gameo.org/encyclopedia/contents/W39.html>

Third Way Café. Third Way Media. <www.thirdway.com>

Wenger, John C. and Elmer S. Yoder. "Prayer Veil." *Global Anabaptist Mennonite Encyclopedia Online*. 1989. Global Anabaptist Mennonite Encyclopedia Online. Retrieved 21 February 2009 <www.gameo.org/encyclopedia/contents/P739ME.html>

THE AUTHOR

Jodi Nisly Hertzler, born in Atlanta, Georgia, was uprooted at three months to join Reba Place Fellowship, an intentional community in Evanston, Illinois. Her family lived there until she was seven (long enough for the words *cooperation* and *community* to become permanently etched in her brain), when her parents decided that they didn't want their children to experience only city life.

So she and her brother were thrust into the antithesis of so-called city life by a move to a West Virginia home lacking in electricity, plumbing, and reliable kitchen floors (it didn't stay that way for long but was quite the adventure while it lasted). The family lived in West Virginia for six years, attending a Church of the Brethren congregation before moving to Harrisonburg, Virginia.

Jodi graduated from Eastern Mennonite University with a degree in English because she loved literature and fancied herself an adequate writer; she didn't declare a minor because she couldn't commit to one. Feeling a distinct lack of direction, she tried various jobs: as a university secretary, an interior design assistant, a nursery worker (plants, not children), and a special education assistant at a middle school. For two years she and husband Shelby led a Service Adventure unit in Albany, Oregon.

Eventually, they started a family, and Jodi shelved the search for a career to concentrate on her children. After moving back to Virginia, she started working for Mennonite Media, now Third Way Media, from home, answering online questions about Mennonites. Now the mother of three, she remains lacking in focus career-wise, but continues her e-mail ministry among the demands of family and community life. Jodi and Shelby built a home in Harrisonburg, Virginia, and are active members at Community Mennonite Church.